Contents

What are diggers?

Diggers are earth-moving machines.
They come in all shapes and sizes.

Some enormous diggers are
used for digging deep pits in the
ground. Other diggers are small
and can be used in the garden.

4

Different diggers are used for different types of jobs all over the world. They travel over rough, rocky ground and through thick mud. Diggers climb up steep slopes and work at the top of high mounds of earth.

Digger fact!
Some diggers dance to music. 'Dancing diggers' perform at shows in front of cheering crowds!

Diggers are used in **construction**, and also in road building. They can even help out in emergencies!

Parts of the digger

There are different types of digger. Look at all the different parts. Do you know what they are all for?

This is an excavator.

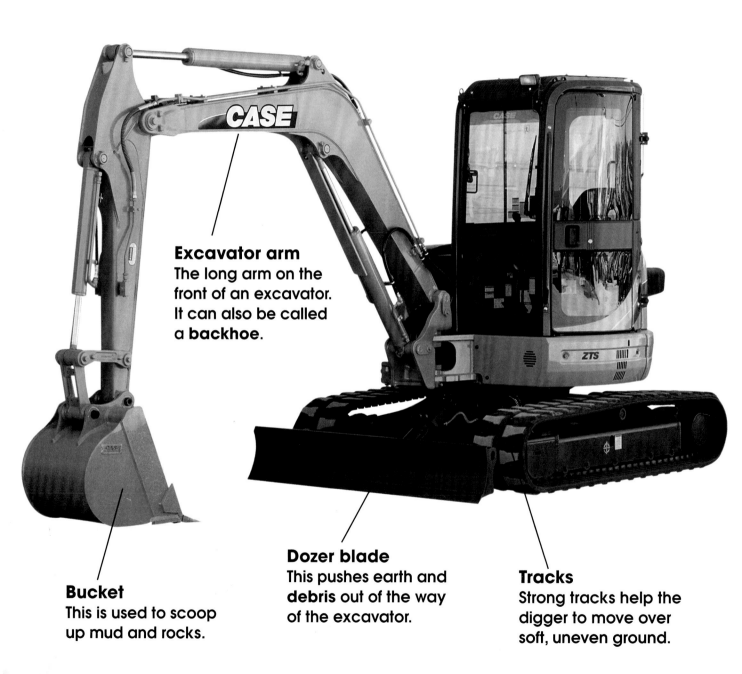

Excavator arm
The long arm on the front of an excavator. It can also be called a **backhoe**.

Bucket
This is used to scoop up mud and rocks.

Dozer blade
This pushes earth and **debris** out of the way of the excavator.

Tracks
Strong tracks help the digger to move over soft, uneven ground.

6

Digger fact!
People first started using diggers more than 200 years ago.

This is a loader.

Engine
The digger has a powerful engine.

Lights

Cab
The digger **operator** sits in the cab.

Loader
Two arms attached to the front of the digger.

Steps

Wheels
Big wheels help the digger to travel over any kind of ground.

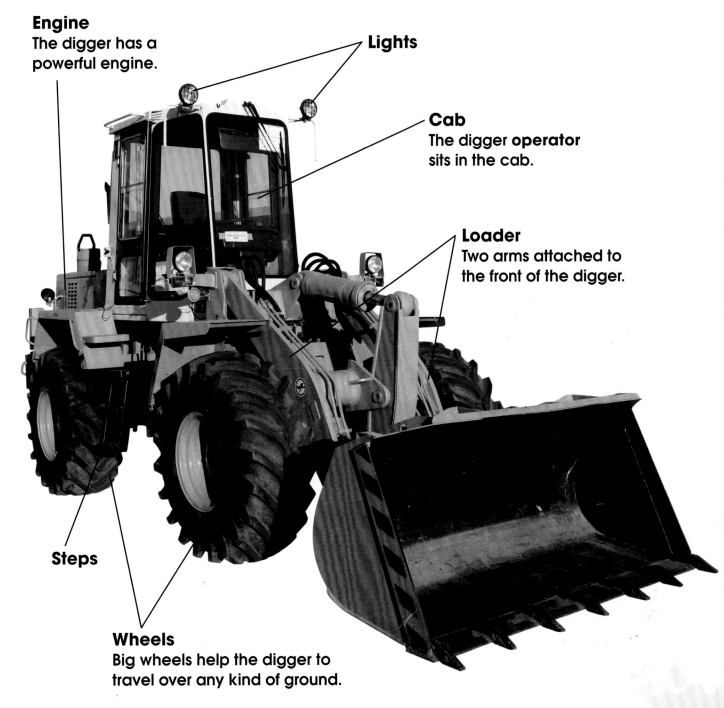

Wheels and tracks

Diggers are very heavy. They need big wheels to carry them along. The wheels at the front are used to **steer** the digger. The wheels at the back help to push the digger along.

Lugs

The wheels are covered in thick tyres that are made from rubber. The tyres have deep bumps on them called **lugs**. The lugs help the wheels to grip the ground.

8

Some diggers have tracks instead of wheels. These are sometimes known as **crawlers**. Each track is stretched around two wheels.

Tracks

Tracks

The engine turns the wheels and this moves the tracks. Tracks help to spread out the digger's weight so that it does not sink into soft ground.

Digger fact!

Crawler tracks work like skis. If you stand on skis you don't sink into soft snow. So, if a digger stands on tracks it won't sink into the mud!

9

Inside the digger

The person who drives the digger is called the operator. The operator sits in the cab. The cab has big windows so that the operator can see all around.

Most diggers have two sets of controls. One set is used to run the engine and drive the machine along. The other set is used to control the equipment on the front or back.

Engine

The digger's engine runs on fuel. It is similar to a car engine, but much bigger and much more powerful. Power from the engine is used to drive the digger along and to work the equipment.

Digger fact!
Before the engines that we use today were invented, diggers were powered by **steam engines**.

Loaders

Loaders have two arms. These are attached to the front of the digger. The arms can move up high in the air or down low to the ground. A big bucket is attached to the end of the arms.

Bucket

First the operator moves the bucket down so that it is on the ground. Then the digger moves forwards and scoops up a load. The arms tilt the bucket up, and lift it high up in the air.

12

When the arms are up in the air, the digger operator can drive along and carry the load somewhere else. The arms tip the bucket down to empty the load.

Digger fact!
Some loaders can carry 38 tonnes – that's the same weight as 38 cars.

Excavators

An excavator is a digger with a long arm attached to the front. The arm has a joint in the middle, just like your elbow. The arm can move up, down and to each side.

Digger fact!
Some excavators have extra-long arms — they can stretch up to 25 metres.

14

A bucket is attached to the arm. The operator moves the arm out and down, so that the bucket is on the ground. Then the operator scrapes the bucket along the ground and scoops up earth or rocks.

The operator twists the excavator around, and drops the earth away from the hole.

Most excavators can turn a full circle on their base.

Backhoe loaders

The backhoe loader is a very clever digger. It has a loader attached to the front and an excavator arm, or backhoe, attached to the back.

Backhoe

Loader

Stabilizer leg

Backhoe loaders have **stabiliser legs**. This helps to make sure the digger is stable when the backhoe is being used.

16

Digger fact!
The backhoe loader was originally adapted from the tractor!

In the cab of a backhoe loader there are two sets of equipment controls, as well as a set of driving controls. One set controls the loader and the other set controls the backhoe.

Stabiliser legs

The operator's seat can spin around to face either set of controls.

17

The bucket

An important **attachment** for a digger is the bucket. Loaders use buckets to lift up and carry heavy loads, such as earth or gravel.

Bucket

Excavators use buckets to scoop things up. Buckets are made of metal and are very strong.

Digger fact!
There are more than 50 different types of bucket.

18

Some buckets have teeth that cut into the ground and break it up so that the excavator can lift it.

Teeth

Some buckets are very small. A small digger might use a small, narrow bucket to cut a long, thin trench in the ground for a cable or pipe.

19

Attachments

Diggers can do more than just digging holes or lifting earth. To do different jobs the operator can use different attachments.

auger

The operator could use an **auger** to make a deep hole in the ground. This looks like a big, metal drill. When the auger is pushed into the ground, it spins and makes a hole.

Digger fact!

There are all sorts of digger attachments. There is even a big magnet that can pick up scrap metal, and steel cutters that can snip up metal!

20

A **hammer** is a hard, metal spike. It moves very quickly up and down. When it hammers against a solid surface, such as concrete or rock, it breaks it up into small pieces.

Hammer

Other attachments are used for lifting. A grab attachment can be used to pick up logs.

Grab

21

A team of diggers

Different diggers work together in teams. One digger might use a hammer to break up hard rock.

Dumper truck

A loader or excavator tips mud and rocks into the back of a **dumper truck** so that it can be taken away.

This excavator is digging a deep hole in the ground. It then scoops up mud and rocks from one place and tips them out onto a big pile.

A loader can then shovel up the mud and rocks from the pile into a dumper truck to carry away.

Digger fact!
Another type of digger uses **suction** instead of scooping earth up with a bucket. It works like a huge vacuum cleaner and sucks up mud and other debris.

23

Small diggers

Skid-steer loaders are small loaders. They have two arms, like a big loader, but instead of sticking out in front, the arms are either side of the cab.

They can work in much tighter spaces than a big loader. They have four small wheels that are all the same size.

Mini-diggers are small versions of the excavator. They are lighter than big diggers and their cab and engine are much smaller.

Most mini-diggers can spin around on a small base. Mini-diggers are designed to work on small jobs.

Digger fact!
Some mini-diggers are so small they can fit through doorways.

The biggest diggers

To dig big holes you need a very big digger. Loaders and excavators both come in very large sizes. They are heavier and much more powerful than diggers that you might see being used on a building site.

Digger fact!
Some of the biggest diggers can weigh 13,000 tonnes. That's more than 2,000 elephants!

These machines would tower over the tallest person. They are so big that you need a ladder to get onto them. With their giant buckets, they can move an enormous amount of earth in a very short time.

The biggest diggers are used in mining and quarrying. This is where workers dig up rocks from deep in the ground. To do this, they need powerful machines.

27

Special diggers

One specialised digging machine is called a bucket-wheel excavator. This uses a big wheel with buckets on it. As the wheel turns, the buckets dig into the ground and fill with earth.

Wheel with buckets

Dragline excavators can also be used to dig immense holes. These pull a heavy metal bucket across the ground using a thick, wire rope.

Digger fact!
The biggest dragline excavator that was ever built was called 'Big Muskie'. It was used in the coal industry in Ohio, USA. It took three years to build.

Some diggers are made to work in water. These are called **dredgers**. They scoop or suck up sand and mud from the sea floor. Some dredgers are mounted on boats and some are mounted on platforms above the water.

29

Digger activities

History: Think of all the jobs that diggers do. How were these jobs done years ago, before diggers were invented?

Geography: Diggers are used all over the world. In which countries do you think the biggest diggers are used?

Science: What makes some diggers more powerful than others?

Literacy: How do you think houses are built? Write a short story about a construction site. Think about the different jobs that each digger does and include them in your story.

Design & Technology: Make a digger out of different materials. What important things do you have to consider when making the attachments?

30

Glossary

attachment a piece of equipment that is fixed to a digger to do a particular job

auger a drill attachment that is used to make a hole in the ground

backhoe the excavator arm on a backhoe loader

construction building structures such as houses, schools and offices

crawler a machine that has tracks instead of wheels

debris loose material

dredger a type of digger that scoops up mud or sand from a river or sea bed

dumper truck a truck used to carry rocks and earth from one place to another

excavator arm the long arm on an excavator that is used to do many jobs, such as digging holes

hammer a tool that can be attached to an excavator arm. It is used to break up hard surfaces

lugs deep bumps on a tyre

operator a person who drives a digger and controls the equipment

stabilizer legs supports that stop a backhoe loader wobbling about

steam engine an engine that is powered by steam

steer to make a vehicle go in a particular direction

suction a vacuum of air that pulls things towards it

Further information

Big Trucks and Diggers in 3-D (Caterpillar), Mark Blum, Chronicle Books, 2001.

Digger (Machines at Work), Dorling Kindersley, 2005.

Diggers (Big Machines), David and Penny Glover, Franklin Watts, 2008.

Diggers (On the Go), David and Penny Glover, Wayland, 2007.

Diggers and Cranes (Young Machines), C Young, Usborne Publishing Ltd., 2004.

Diggers and Dumpers Ultimate Sticker Book, Dorling Kindersley, 2005.

This is my Digger (Mega Machine Drivers), Chris Oxlade, Franklin Watts, 2006.

Trucks and Diggers (Wild About), Caroline Bingham, Ticktock Media Ltd., 2003.

Index